W9-BMZ-776

A Time Saving Summary of David Allen's
Book on Productivity:

Getting Things Done

by Shortcut Summaries

Published by CornerTrade Publishing,
a subsidiary of CornerTrade, LLC

DEDICATION

This book is dedicated to all those who have too much stuff in their lives, too many great ideas to develop, and too little time to get it all done.

CONTENTS

ACKNOWLEDGMENTS

Introduction

Summary of David Allen's *Getting Things Done*

Overwhelmed by work? Stressed out and unable to think clearly about even the simplest of tasks? Well, you are not alone. Packed inside this book is our summary of David Allen's tips and strategies for transforming that muddled, over-worked mind into an efficient, smoothly operating machine.

Allen's concept seems almost too simple to work — but that's precisely why we think it does work. Using what you'll learn here, you'll be able to harness the power of your mind. You'll streamline your work habits by using the fastest and most efficient computer known to man — the human brain.

How Work Has Changed - Why We Need a New Approach

The major difference between the working worlds of today versus yesteryear is the wealth of information available to us, and the speed at which we can access that information. While this information explosion is a wonderful thing if used properly, it can also overload our brains before we even realize what's happening.

How we think is the other major reason why we feel drowned by a sea of tasks. Most of us never learned how to think about work in a relaxed manner. Due to technology, this is a skill that's more crucial than ever before. Thankfully, it's a skill which *can* be easily learned.

Section 1 - The Basics of Getting Things Done

Two Main Goals

If you've already reached critical mass in terms of work overload, you may be feeling as though it's literally impossible to accomplish everything you want to do in a relaxed manner. Take a deep breath, because it *is* possible.

The techniques you're about to learn are things you're already familiar with. What you're going to learn is simply how to organize these processes into a system which you can put your trust in, a system which lets your mind deal with things efficiently and in a relaxed manner.

There are two main goals here. That's all, just two goals – simple enough, right? Master these, and you'll notice a positive change immediately.

1. Collect all your tasks – large or small, crucial or mundane – into an *external* organizational system which you trust implicitly.

2. Implement strict (yet relaxed) self-discipline. The moment a new task presents itself, you must learn to make decisions regarding that task. Those decisions will then be moved to your organizational system, where they can't clog your brain. Training yourself to do this *every time* a new tasks pops up takes some practice, but the payoff is huge.

Understanding Why – What's Really Going On?

Do you know anybody who feels like they're truly on top of things? Probably not. It's a rare feeling these days.

A big part of this is that the nature of work has shifted. We no longer have the luxury of boundaries. When we finish with our workday, we bring all our technology home with us. Our jobs are less about doing, and more about thinking.

Another key component is the fact that the workplace has changed in many ways. You probably perform many tasks which are not covered by your job title. This is the new normal, one that can drive us crazy if we don't change how we approach our jobs.

Businesses have changed as well. Technology altered the work world forever. People switch careers many times during their lives. We're constantly in a state of improving, moving forward, and pressing on.

What's the result? We never (or hardly ever) devote our full attention to the task at hand. We also deny ourselves the chance to feel as though we've done a good job, since most of us question what could have been done better.

Information flies at us from every angle, and our minds are constantly creating new ideas and tasks at the same time. Every single one of these items brings with it an even longer list of "what if" questions. Exhausted? It's no wonder.

Tackling a Job with the Wrong Tools

We were not raised to handle this level of information overload. Our parents did not have to deal with anything close to it. Would you, ten years ago, have been able to conceive of the lightning-fast world in which you now work every day? Probably not.

This is a new world, a new reality. Sadly, too many of us are trying to conquer it using tools we picked up when things were much simpler. What you're about to learn is how to create new tools. They're not elaborate or difficult tools to create – simply different ones. A different world requires a different type of thinking in order to succeed.

Our Outdated Tools

Two main schools of thought have dominated the working world for years. One is the philosophy of keeping our minds focused on a broad picture of what we want to accomplish. Avoid getting bogged down in the mundane detail of a task, and keep your eye on the prize.

The main flaw with this type of thinking is the simple fact that mundane details are a huge part of any project. Lofty goals can't be accomplished without taking care of the details, and so leaving details entirely out of your thought process simply won't work.

The other major school of thought is the detail-oriented school, the school which insists that a well-stocked calendar, priority list and to-do list can simplify even the most complicated workday.

As with broad, visionary thinking, this method has its good points as well. In fact, you'll learn that tools such as these are a key part of changing how you think. However, they can't do it all by themselves. Our days are subject to interruption from many different sources. A very popular – and outdated – idea told us that every item on our mental list should be prioritized.

This simply doesn't apply to most jobs anymore. In today's society, we operate under the unspoken notion that *everything* is a priority, and leaving even one small detail off the list is viewed as lazy.

Lists have their place, but that place is within a more structured organizational system. Go ahead and make a list if you'd like. Yes, right now. Take a few minutes to write down every single detail, every item that needs your attention. Leave nothing out. When you're done, your eyes may pop out of your skull...it's essentially impossible. You can't get it all done, and so you feel like a failure.

An Athletic Approach to Success

For centuries, athletes all around the world have recognized the phenomenon known as "the zone." In eastern cultures, it was and is considered necessary to achieve a state of mental stillness, readiness and calm alertness in order to master the martial arts. Western athletes often stumble into the zone quite accidentally, but spend most of their time trying to get back into this blissful state of relaxed focus.

You're learning how to create your own zone. A state of mind in which you are aware, alert and productive, yet calm and relaxed. You don't stress in the zone – you simply *do*. The zone is not some unattainable Nirvana – it can be cultivated with remarkable simplicity, once a person understands how to organize their thoughts and take decisive action.

Certainly, this is better than a non-stop (figurative, literal or a bit of both) caffeine rush followed by a confused, unproductive crash. Yet the latter is how many of us live our lives, thinking that we're not good enough because we can't climb to the top of that endless heap of projects and conquer them all.

Finding your zone will show you that you can get things done, with efficiency and effectiveness, without going crazy.

We tend to react in an inappropriate manner to many of our workday concerns. Overreacting, by becoming anxious or reaching for yet another espresso shot, is not productive. Productivity and unmanageable stress can't coexist. Once we've reached a state of burnout, we often don't react enough. Blearily focused on what absolutely *must* be accomplished in order to avoid being fired or losing our companies, we cast everything else aside. Neither extreme is productive.

Appropriate reactions are one of the major keys to working – and living – in your own personal zone. An organizational system which you trust makes it possible to react appropriately. In fact, it makes it easy!

Tying Up Loose Ends

Everything we need to do but haven't done yet is constantly being evaluated by our subconscious. If we take an item, process it and either complete it or place it in our organizational system, our subconscious can relax and allow us to focus on the task in front of us.

Think of these unfinished, unsorted items as loose ends. Loose ends can be as big as expanding your business, and they can be as small as remembering to pick up bread on your way home from work.

There are three very simple actions that need to be used with every item. Once you've practiced for a very short time, these steps will come to you quickly and naturally.

First, you need to get the item out of your mind and into your organizational system. This can be as simple as a to-do list, but it can also be a multi-faceted approach involving your computer's various organizing apps, your smartphone, a tablet – literally anything that works for you is just fine. If you don't fully trust your system, however, your subconscious will keep chewing on those items.

Secondly, review each item and make a note of what needs to be done about it. What is the next step?

Third comes action. Once all these items have been processed and organized, you must review them regularly to ensure progress. This could mean each morning, twice a day or even every hour.

Pop Quiz!

Don't get nervous. We're just going to rehearse the sorting and organizing process. Choose an issue which is on your mind. Any issue will work just fine. Now, figure out what the next step would be. To solve or move forward with this issue, what needs to be done next? Not every step, just the next step.

Knowing the next step, for the majority of people, is a huge relief in and of itself. This wonderful feeling of being in control can grow and expand until it is your regular routine, not just a singular moment.

Working Our Brains Harder Than Ever

Our current workplace atmosphere has shifted dramatically into what is known as knowledge work. Knowledge work simply means that fewer jobs are based on physical work and more are based on mental work.

Knowledge work is not inherently bad; on the contrary, it is necessary and has led to some amazing innovations. However, it is not the type of work our brains are programmed to perform. Generation upon generation engaged in physical labor to earn a living. Sure, they had to think...but it was very clear thinking, regarding the job at hand. When that was done, they moved on to the next job.

Today's knowledge work can seem endless. Since we can always be thinking, regardless of whatever else we're physically doing, a vast number of people are literally *always working*.

Emptying Your Mind

Things stay on our minds because they haven't been properly processed. By learning how to create an organizational system which you trust, you'll see that things can be sorted, organized and put aside until later very effectively. The trick is ensuring that your subconscious trusts the system. Our subconscious minds do what we tell them, to an amazing extent. This is part of the reason why positive thinking can have such amazing results. Checking and reorganizing this system, as needed, is also crucial.

The real work comes in the form of action, not thought. Unless your task is to brainstorm ideas, or something similar, thinking does very little. In fact, it can be a hindrance to productivity.

Processing your thoughts into necessary actions is the first step toward a relaxed and empty mind, one which is ready to tackle whatever you choose. Your thoughts need to be dealt with, but the way to deal with them is to turn them into actions. This will give you a greater sense of control, which many people find comes amazingly quickly after processing just a few nagging thoughts.

The action which corresponds to each thought, item or project needs to be placed in your organizational system, whatever that might be. For example, if you have a party coming up that you can't get off your mind, figure out the next step. Once you turn those vague, nagging thoughts into actions, and you file those actions into your system, your mind will breathe a sigh of relief and you'll be able to focus on the task at hand.

Horizontal and Vertical Thinking

Understanding the two major ways in which our minds monitor our environments is a crucial part of constructing an organizational system you trust. We think in two ways: horizontally and vertically.

Horizontal thinking is the broad picture of your life. You've seen security cameras in stores, panning back and forth to capture images of a broad space. Your mind does the same thing.

Vertical thinking is more focused. Let's say that security camera is motion-activated during hours when the store is closed. If it detects movement, it stops and zooms in to take a closer look at whatever is happening. Our minds do this when we focus on an issue.

Both types of mental processing can quickly lead to muddled overload if our thoughts are not processed quickly and neatly. Creating your system of organization will allow you to quickly process all the items your mind picks up horizontally, creating a clean and neat vertical "file" for you to review.

This absolutely must occur outside your mind...keeping things in your head is unproductive, confusing to the subconscious and leads to disorganized thinking. Remember that any system will work, as long as it is *external* and – this is the big one – you trust it implicitly. The third key is to check and review the system regularly.

Living in a Fog

So many of us haven't implemented an effective organizational system, and live under a constant fog of muddled thoughts, that we barely know any other way to live. If you're like most, you'll be amazed at the difference you feel after implementing your new tools, and you'll wonder how you've survived all these years of foggy thinking.

Creating Your Personal Organizing Method

Creating a method for organizing your thoughts and actions depends on five key stages. In this section we'll review these stages, giving you guidelines for creating your own. Remember that trusting your system is essential, so don't feel pressured to use a particular tool if it really doesn't work for you.

You'll need to use or create a system which allows you to move between these stages quickly and easily: Collecting information; Processing that information; Organizing the processed results; Reviewing those results; Taking action.

Do not feel overwhelmed by these steps. This might seem like a lot to take in. However, remember that you're learning an entirely new way to process information. It will take a bit of time to get used to performing these steps on each new item that comes your way, but soon it will become second nature.

The good news is that once you begin, you'll feel an immediate heightened sense of control and relaxation. This will give you the motivation you need to implement these steps on a regular basis, and once done regularly, they will become as natural for you as breathing.

Collection Basics

While some items are already collected for you (such as emails), you must collect others in some type of system which you create yourself. This can involve several tools. You may choose notebooks or legal pads, a physical in-box which sits on your desk, a note-taking application on your smartphone or tablet, or even a voice recorder. Whatever works best for you is fine.

Once your method is chosen, it must be organized and accessible. Collect everything, from work projects to shopping lists. Don't allow a single bit of input to enter your brain without collecting it somewhere *outside* of your brain.

as many collection tools as you need. Having too many tools is simply another roadblock to clear thinking. .... how many you truly need in order to be fully organized, and use only that number. Of course, remember to review and empty your collection tools regularly in order to keep your system flowing and functioning properly.

Processing Basics

Once you've collected an item, you will process it. Following is a step-by-step format you can follow for most items, allowing you to think clearly and keep organized.

Is this something you can take action on? If the answer is no, you have three choices. You can throw it in the garbage. You can save it for reference (take-out menus are a great example). You can file it away for later review.

If the answer is yes, you have more choices. Can this be completed in less than two minutes? Do it. Right now. Don't waste time.

Many items will, of course, take longer. Determine the next step for your item. If it's something which can be passed on to an assistant, do that immediately. Remember that delegating isn't just for work...it can mean asking your son to run to the store for bread.

If you must attend to an item yourself, determine the first (or next) step, and then write the steps down on a calendar or other tool which you can easily review.

Congratulations...your item has been processed!

Organizing Basics

Your organizational system will now collect your processed information. Transfer your steps, or next steps, into a tool you trust. If something has a deadline, put it on a calendar. If not, place it in a file which contains important items with no definite time constraints. Remember to trust your system implicitly and review it regularly. A calendar won't do you much good if you review it sporadically.

Depending on how busy you are, you may need a calendar that offers you a week at a glance, a month at a glance, or one which breaks the day down into hours or even fifteen-minute increments. Remember, it's all about what works best for you.

You should have one "master list," containing all of your loose ends, regardless of size or importance. This will allow you to see all of your "to-do" items at a glance. It at all possible, make this master list portable, so you can review it anytime, anywhere. A tablet or smartphone note-taking app is ideal, although a notebook will also work well as long as you remember to keep it with you at all times.

If you're like many people, you'll most likely end up with at least five sections to your organizational system. Your calendar will keep you on top of projects with a due date. Your master list will keep everything in one place for easy review. Your list of "next steps" will give you concrete actions to take.

In addition to these, you'll need something to contain your less critical but still important items. A list of large projects is essential for many people. This list allows you to view ongoing projects, things which take up more time and have many steps. The reference materials for these projects should be organized elsewhere. Labeled binders are one option.

A list containing vague ideas and fun items is also important. Remember that every single thought is processed by the subconscious until it's dealt with. Is there a list of movies you've been meaning to rent? Write them down. Nothing is too small or unimportant to organize.

Reviewing Basics

Review regularly. Your calendar will be reviewed most often, since these items have deadlines. Check it as often as needed to feel in control. Your master list should be reviewed very regularly as well.

Do a complete review of every single portion of your system once a week. This will keep you on top of things and prevent overload. Move things as needed, complete small tasks, and toss out unnecessary reference materials. Think of your system as an air filter which needs to be cleaned regularly in order to function efficiently. Doing this weekly is much more effective than doing it whenever things become overwhelming...you can *prevent* them from getting overwhelming by being proactive.

"Doing" Basics

Once you're ready to tackle something, take a look at your surroundings. Some things can only be done at home; some require you to be at the office. Wherever you are when you decide to work, choose items which can be done where you are right now.

How much energy do you have? How much time is available to you? If you can't get it done (even a step), don't start it. Move on to a step which you have the time and energy to complete. Pushing yourself too hard will only lead to overload.

How important is this step? Move time-sensitive items to the top of the list. Once those are out of the way, you can concentrate on important items which don't have time constraints.

Following these priorities will allow you to put more trust in your choice of actions, which clears your mind out and allows you to relax, knowing that things have been done properly. When an action is completed, remember to remove it from your system and move the next step forward. Don't let an item idle in your system once it's completed.

Five Organized Stages to Planning a Project

In order to be highly effective, there are two main objectives which must be the focus of any project planning endeavor. One of these is a very clear picture of the desired outcome. Next, but just as important, are steps and reminders which have been placed in a trusted system of organization.

In this section, you'll be introduced to five essential stages in planning a project. You'll also learn why so many planning efforts fail. If you feel a bit overwhelmed at any point, remember that these steps sound much more involved and difficult than they truly are, and that near-immediate results are a frequent occurrence!

Productive Vertical Thinking

Horizontal thinking is an important component of planning. However, planning a specific project must include some focused vertical thinking. The end result of this vertical thinking should not be to hurry through it – this results in lost ideas. The desired result should be an organized list of next steps, which will get the project moving, give you actionable items to work on and, most importantly, get it *out of your brain* so it can't interfere with other necessary tasks.

Forcing Our Brains to Work against Nature

There is a way our brains naturally work. There is also a way we've been taught, by well-meaning teachers and professors. Working against nature is simply unproductive. Why not take our brain's natural method and run with it?

In a relaxed setting with no looming deadlines, our minds naturally go through five general stages of planning.

1. Defining the purpose comes first. Let's say you're planning an office party. Your purpose was the reason for the party, and that reason flipped your brain into planning mode. Whether it's celebrating a co-worker's birthday, reaching a sales goal or opening a new store, that urge to celebrate is your purpose.

2. Visualizing the outcome is next. You probably see a room full of happy, laughing people, socializing and snacking on some tasty finger-foods. Your purpose is your *why,* while your visualization is your *what.* What do you want to create? A fun, relaxed celebration.

3. Brainstorming is the next natural stage. Since this party is not planned yet, our brains begin to fill in the space between then and now. We wonder what day might be best...a day when everybody will be relaxed. If the party will be outdoors, of course we consider the weather. Should we serve a full meal or only snacks? Which tasks can be delegated, and which do we want to be fully in charge of? Brainstorming is unstructured problem-solving. These thoughts seem random, but they are valuable and should be noted down as soon as possible to avoid losing a great idea.

4. Next comes organization, in which we take our brainstorming ideas and break them down. "Well, it looks like Wednesday will be sunny and pleasant, great party weather!" Organization is focused thinking regarding the thoughts we captured during brainstorming.

5. "Next Steps" are the last stage. We have organized our brainstorming, now is the time to break that organization down into actionable items. Once all these next steps have been organized in your system, the party is "taken care of", in the sense that everything necessary has been processed and organized. Your brain can now move on to other tasks.

Action, Not Reaction

When we force the outline model of thinking, we often end up in a panic. All that time spent creating outlines leaves us scrambling, at the last minute, to come up with actionable steps. Ironically, this is often the time when somebody speaks up and says "Hold it! What are we actually trying to accomplish here?"

This question, regardless of how it's stated, usually jolts the group into action. It also starts the group thinking in a much more natural way and – surprise – things actually get accomplished!

If you're going to revert back to the natural way our minds work anyway, why not do it from the beginning? Not only will you save time, but you'll save your sanity.

Examining the Five Stages

Clarifying these stages a bit will help you to implement them more easily. We'll also touch on the most important parts of each stage.

Purpose and Principles

Remember that this is your *why*. Realizing *why* you are doing something is actually the most important clue you have as to *how* that something should be done.

Realizing, clearly and with focus, why you are doing something, regardless of how big or small, gives you a much simpler route to the best next steps.

Several other things are clarified by asking why. It creates specific criteria you can use in making decisions. It gives you a clearer picture of a successful outcome. It can clarify potential resources and options. It makes your focus much easier to visualize and, perhaps most importantly, it motivates you. After all, if you don't have a clear picture of success in your mind, how on earth can your project be successful?

If you find yourself stuck at any point during project planning, go back to your original purpose. Once you weigh options against your clear, focused purpose and the principles which guide that purpose, decisions usually become much easier to make.

Visualizing Your Outcome

Remember that the outcome is your *what*. The power behind this step is brilliantly simple. What will this particular project look like, once it has been completed successfully? What will the very best outcome look like?

Don't worry about all the steps to get you there. Simply visualizing your outcome is a huge part of making that outcome a reality.

Brainstorming

It's very hard to keep your mind focused for more than a minute without some concrete visual reference points. This is why collecting your brainstorming ideas is so important. It doesn't matter if they're messy...most people's are...what matters is collecting those ideas the moment they occur.

Here are some keys to effective brainstorming:

1. Don't criticize or judge your Ideas
2. This is the time for quantity; forget quality.
3. Do not analyze.

Following these easy and natural steps will lead to the most effective brainstorming you've possibly ever done!

Organizing

This, of course, is taking what you've come up with and translating it into an actionable set of plans. Follow the steps of *Identifying what's important; Sorting what's important;* and *Clarifying details.* Don't make this harder than it is – essentially all you're doing is clearing out the "junk" ideas and streamlining the good ones.

Next Steps

As we've discussed, a next step is the *very next step* you need to take on any particular part of a project plan. If you need to make a phone call, delegate the activity to somebody else, or flesh out an idea a bit more, write it down.

If you find yourself thinking about the project in a befuddled manner, it probably means you need to review and clarify one or more of these steps. Once everything is broken into actionable steps, your subconscious will rest.

If the project still seems unclear, move your thinking upward and review your purpose, principles and visualization. You could even brainstorm again. If you feel that not enough is being done, move your thinking down and review your organization or next steps.

What's Next?

As you can see, these steps are wonderfully simple. They work well with the way your mind naturally functions. This means that right now, right this second, you have the power and ability to streamline your life!

However, sometime we all need a little push, or a little encouragement. You'll find that in Section 2 of this summary, along with tricks and tips to get you started toward a life in your zone.

Section 2 - Practicing Productivity Without Stress

Start With the Right Tools

Your very first step in creating your zone is setting up an efficient workspace. This is actually a method of "tricking" yourself into being productive. Think about it...when you change clothes after work, those comfortable sweats cue your body that it's time to relax. The same is true of work clothes, workout gear, and other types of clothing.

Creating a workspace is governed by the same principle. In this section, we'll review the most important steps for creating a workspace which allows you to implement your organizational system in a fun, relaxed and productive manner.

Two days is considered the optimal amount of time for getting this done. If you're setting up satellite workstations at home or for on-the-go productivity, set aside time for these as well.

If you consider your time and work split evenly between your home and office workstations, create identical systems for each. These systems should be interchangeable and accessible. Using a fully portable laptop, with upgraded memory to handle the extra information, is ideal for many.

Pay Attention to the Home Office

Even if you spend most of your time working in another location, your home office should be as easy to use and efficient as the desk you sit down to at work each day.

An On-The-Go Work Station

Carry only as much as you need to accomplish your most common tasks, and ensure that your on-the-go system is as easy to use as possible.

Forget the Shared Office

While many couples think they can work in the same home office, at the same desk, on the same computer, this arrangement very rarely works. Set up your own space, even if it means sacrificing size. Better to have a small, dedicated workspace than to lose valuable time or ideas because your spouse is already using the home office.

What You Need

Flat, Open Trays - These will serve as a physical in-box, a place for in-progress papers and a resting spot for items which need to be filed. Three is considered minimal. If you can, look for the kind that stacks in order to save space.

Stapler, Tape, Rubber Bands - Organizing occurs in steps. If you jot down a great idea only to have it fly off your desk and into the garbage, you're out of luck. Collect similar items and secure them as often as necessary.

Blank Paper - Old-school as it seems, this is a highly effective way of capturing thoughts. Use whatever size works for you, whether that is typing paper, yellow legal pads or pink sticky notes.

Labeling Tool - Look for one which creates bold, white-on-black labels. You will use this for files, binders and many other things that will surprise you. Nearly everyone who begins to use a labeling tool is amazed at just how much a simple tool can streamline their workdays.

Calendar - For now, stick with the calendar you're already using. Later on, we'll discuss ways of determining how to choose the most effective calendar for you. Remember that a calendar can't be your entire system, but it's an essential component.

Organizer - Choosing an organizer is a very personal decision. Today's sophisticated smartphones are wonderfully efficient at organizing your thoughts while keeping them close at hand, accessible, portable and changeable.

File Folders - You'll want a good supply of plain manila folders which are easy to label.

Garbage/Recycling - This is most important during the initial two-day organizational period. You'll probably be amazed at just how much stuff you don't really need. During regular office use, having a garbage or recycling container handy makes you more likely to use it, rather than let papers pile up on your desk.

Pens/Pencils/Sharpener - Keep them handy, sharp and ready to use.

Filing Basics

Far too many people make filing more complicated than it needs to be. All you need is a high-quality cabinet, a large supply of files and a labeling tool.

Keep it Handy - Whether you need one file drawer or six, keep them within reach of your desk.

Keep it Easy - Forget about color-coding or other complicated methods of filing. A-Z is the easiest and most efficient method of filing in existence. The only exception to this rule would be a truly huge amount of paperwork on a *single topic*. This instance would benefit from its own dedicated file drawer.

Keep it Streamlined - In filing, this refers to keeping each drawer less than ¾ full. The reason for this is subconscious. If your drawers are stuffed full, taking things out is a hassle, and putting new stuff in is difficult.

You are now equipped with all you need to implement a new, organized method of thinking and working!

Collecting Everything

Now that you have all the supplies you need, we'll take a closer look at the best way to collect all your "stuff." That includes *everything*. Remember that every loose end is a hindrance to productivity.

Depending on a variety of factors, this process can take from one to six hours; more time will be needed if you undertake a full-scale purging and organization of not only your office but other areas of your life.

Keeping every aspect of your life under control all of the time simply isn't logical. However, it's a great ideal to work toward. Even if you never reach it, the goal will keep you motivated to routinely clear out and organize your life and your thinking.

Why It's Smart

There are three main reasons for collecting all your stuff before beginning to process and deal with it. Knowing how much you have gives you a sense of control. It also gives you a concrete stopping point; when you process it all, you'll be done. Last, it frees your mind.

Even if you don't tackle it all at once, simply knowing that all your "stuff" is collected somewhere can allow you to concentrate on other tasks. Otherwise, part of your subconscious is always going to be contemplating that unknown blob of stuff crammed into your bottom desk drawer.

Let's Get Started!

Get yourself a stack of note paper (you'll be taking notes on some items), a pen and a *large* in-box. This in-box will be much larger than the one that will routinely sit on your desk; it will be where you collect all your out-of-place items for processing.

A main goal is to train your mind to notice what's out of place immediately. Start right now.

For most people, there will be four categories of items which don't need action.

Office & Other Supplies
Reference & Resource Materials
Adornments & Decorations
Office & Other Equipment

Keep in mind that simply because an item falls into one of these categories doesn't mean that it's not actionable. Letting that dead, withered plant linger on your windowsill isn't brightening anybody's day. Toss it, and make a note to buy a new one. Put the note in your in-box. Done!

Barriers to Collection

You'll run into several roadblocks. Don't worry; this is normal. Here are the solutions to the most common roadblocks you're likely to encounter.

It's Too Big – If something literally doesn't fit in your in-box (like that dead plant), write it down on something that does. Date the note. In fact, get into the habit of dating all your notes.

There's Too Much – This is very common. Simply stack papers in a pile, being sure to visually distance them from other things and group them together. You'll be processing this first big "purge" very soon, so a few stacks really aren't that big of a deal.

You're Not Sure About Keeping Something – If you really can't decide, keep it and move on. Don't get bogged down trying to decide.

Getting Sidetracked – Another very common occurrence is getting distracted by another task. Forget it for now. You're in collection mode. Everything else can wait.

It's Already Organized – You probably already have a calendar or some type of organizational tool. Since you're starting over, let's really start over. Treat already-organized items as if they just came into your life, and collect them accordingly. This could be represented by a piece of paper with "process smartphone app info" written on it, which would then go in your in-box.

Immediacy – During the course of collection, you might come across something that's fairly urgent. Perhaps a phone call you were supposed to make last week. Ask yourself whether anything truly dire will happen if you let it go. If not, put it in the in-box. If it helps to clarify your thinking, you might create an "emergency" stack of papers for truly immediate tasks.

Your Office

Work in this order:

Desktop or workspace
Desk drawers
Counters
Cabinets
Floor, walls and shelving
Furniture placement

Do you want to change anything? Write it down and put it in the in-box.

Your Home

While your initial collection should target your office, many people find it very helpful to apply these steps to other areas of their life. This includes your home and even your car.

Your Head

Clearing your head is the next step, and should be done with blank paper in front of you. Use a separate piece for each idea; it facilitates brainstorming later on. Go through your mental inventory of tasks, noting each item separately.

What Now?

You probably have a very full in-box and a very empty mind. Congratulations! It seems like a mess now, but this is a crucial step on the way to a streamlined life.

Processing The In-Box

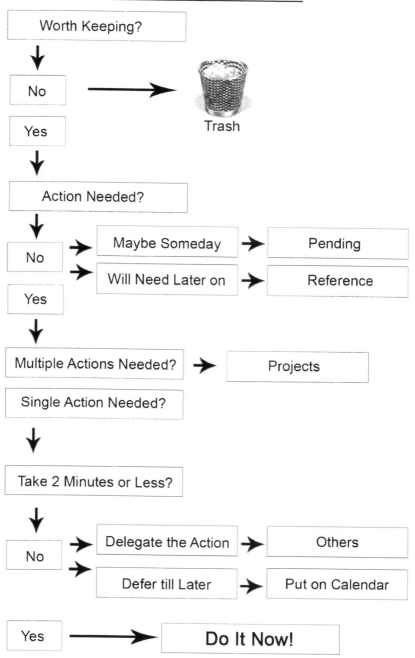

Processing the In-Box

Now that you have a huge stack of papers, your next step is to process that stack. By doing this, you'll accomplish five main goals.

1. Throw away unnecessary or outdated items.
2. Finish any actions taking less than two minutes to accomplish.
3. Delegate anything which can/should be delegated.
4. Organize anything requiring more than two minutes into your trusted organizational system.
5. Clarify larger projects.

As you can see, this section focuses on processing items from your in-box to next-step actions. Don't worry about anything else during this stage.

Before you begin, it's recommended that you read through this section. Knowing all the steps beforehand can save you significant time and prevent skipping between processing and organizing.

Remember that having your ideal organizational system isn't a necessity yet. If you haven't purchased that brand-new smartphone with all the desired apps, don't worry. You can easily transfer all your items and notes into it later. For now, focus on processing.

Effective Processing

Three main objectives will help you keep your focus.

The Item On Top Goes First – Whether it's a note on your huge upcoming meeting or a reminder to buy kitty litter, take the top item first. Don't organize or prioritize.

Singular Processing – Don't grab a stack to process...grab one item, one piece of paper. In most cases, multi-tasking will only slow you down. Remember that each item should only take you a few minutes to process. Anything longer will turn into organizing.

Nothing Returns to the In-Box — As soon as an item leaves the in-box, process it. <u>No exceptions</u>. Putting things back only draws out your processing time.

Determining Next Steps

This is, of course, the whole point of processing. However, there will be some items which don't have a next step. These generally fall into one of the following categories:

Trash: This one's fairly obvious. If something has no use, toss it. If you're not sure, and it takes longer than two minutes to figure it out, it goes in your in-box.

Pending — This refers to items which you may or may not do, use or need. They can be collected in a file marked "pending," they can be placed on your calendar, or they have a list of their own. Use whatever method works best for you, just remember to pick an action and do it — quickly.

Reference — This refers to anything containing information which you'll need later on. Take-out menus, employee information, computer manuals — these are all reference materials. File them and label them immediately.

If something doesn't fall into one of these categories, you'll need to decide on a next step. This is simple and complicated at the same time.

Let's imagine that you need to organize a holiday party. "Organize the party" is *not* an acceptable next step. There are too many loose ends. What is the *very next step?* Figure that out (it still shouldn't take much longer than two minutes), and then either do it (if the step itself takes less than two minutes) or make a note of it in your organizational system of choice.

The first step of party planning, for example, might be to create e-mail invitations for your employees. *That* is an actionable next step, and can go right into your system, to be worked on later.

27

A Little More on Next Steps...

Next steps will always fall into one of three categories.

Do It Now – If something takes less than two minutes, do it. Why waste time?

Delegate the Action – Can this be done acceptably by an assistant or family member? If so, either immediately e-mail or call the person to delegate the task. If this can't be done right away, make an appropriate note to file in your system, reminding yourself to delegate the task at the next opportunity.

Defer – This stack will represent the majority of your in-box items. Most things you have will require more than two minutes and will need to be done by you, and so they will need to be deferred until a later date. Make an appropriate notation in your trusted system and move on. You may create a "pending" stack or file for items like these.

Projects

Projects are items which require more than a single action to complete. You'll have lots of them; don't worry, this is normal. We'll review how to fully deal with them in following sections. For now, get everything processed into the appropriate files and stacks. Remember the "golden rule" of two minutes – amazing things can be accomplished in this tiny amount of time, and it's a great way to keep yourself focused.

You've finished processing! Now let's take a look at your organizational system, making sure that things are ready for effective working and thinking.

Airtight Organization

In order for you to clearly focus on anything...big or small...your organizational system must be airtight. Airtight means that you trust the system, and it can collect every single bit of information in your life. Remember that any loose end is eating away at your subconscious until it has been collected, processed and organized.

Don't feel pressured to create this amazing system overnight. For most people, their perfect system evolves over time.

Your Basic Categories

Depending on your lifestyle and occupation, these may be slightly different. However, the following is a great overall list of the seven most common categories of things to be organized.

- Your Projects List
- Material to Support your Projects
- Calendar (items with a definite due date)
- Lists of Next steps
- "Waiting for something or someone" Lists
- Reference Materials
- Your "Someday" or "Might Do" List

Remember that keeping these categories – and all elements of your system – distinct and separate is absolutely crucial. If they begin to bleed over into each other, confusion is sure to follow.

As overly simplistic as it may sound now, all you truly need for your system to work is lists and folders. Sound crazy? Probably. However, once everything has been processed (which you've already done), all you need to keep track of it all is literally folder space and lists. This can be much more than paper files and folders. How you keep track is up to you. It might mean a digitally organized list on your computer, or an old-school list on a legal pad. Remember that whatever works best for you *is* best for you.

Organizing Your Reminders

Calendar actions should be very clear. Don't clutter up your calendar with things you *want* to get done on a certain date. Save it for things which absolutely *must* be done on a certain date, or things which are *happening* on a certain date regardless of whether you're present or not (such as a child's school play).

Keeping these items clearly defined and separate from the rest of your lists will give you a wonderful concrete schedule to follow. You will fill up your days around these "must do" items, ensuring that you never miss a deadline or worry about missing one.

Once your calendar is properly organized, the vast majority of your remaining items will become "when I have time" items.

Organizing Your "As Soon As I Can Get To It" Items

You probably have a lot of these, but don't panic. Organizing them properly will put everything in perspective.

First, look at how many items you have. Is it under 25? If so, you can probably get by quite well with a single master list. This will greatly simplify things for you, so consider yourself lucky.

Have more than 25 items? You're in good company. Most people do. Your next step is to categorize these items by their context. The following is a good basic list of contexts. Of course, your lifestyle and occupation will cancel out some, and create some new ones as well.

Phone Calls – This list should include every call you need to make. If you have a phone handy, you can work on this list, regardless of where you are.

Computer – Obviously, these tasks require a computer to accomplish. This list should be filled with items that can be done at home, in transit or at work, as long as there is a computer in front of you.

Errands – A portable list, this should include everything you need to grab or do when out and about. If you live in one area and work in another, you may want two errand lists.

Office – These tasks require some type of resources which are only available at your office.

Home – This is not a list of home improvements; it's a list of all tasks which can be worked on or completed while you are at home.

Agendas – These items require a very specific context, and may be lists unto themselves. A great example is a list of topics for an upcoming meeting. You can't work on that list anywhere but at that particular meeting.

Read and Review – Not for books or magazines, but for summaries, reports, employee applications and other items which you must read or review, but will take longer than two minutes.

Your "Waiting for Others" List

If you're like most, some of your actions are simply waiting on others' actions. A great example of this is that proposal you sent out last week. You can't do a thing until you hear back from the client. In order to process and organize this item, simply note it on your waiting list. Simply put, these are actions which are waiting on other people.

Items as Reminders

Some people work most efficiently when they have a concrete reminder. You probably have friends who, instead of paying bills online, still receive paper bills in the mail. This is the same concept.

Sometimes, using an item as its own reminder just makes good sense. For example, if there are trade magazines which you read regularly, put the magazines themselves into your "Read and Review" file. This makes much more sense than creating a separate note which says "Catch up on reading trade magazines."

Creating a file for incoming bills which need be paid, as well as another separate file for other financial papers is a very common and useful organizational tool.

Using E-Mail Wisely

A very simple method of organization is to use the tools which are most likely available on your existing e-mail account(s). Most e-mail servers allow you to create customized files. This is an incredibly efficient way to organize, so why not use it?

Create a file or folder for each category of e-mail. Your list will be unique to you and your life/career. Once your folders are properly set up, going through your e-mails in the morning will be a snap. Each one, with a few exceptions, will be very easy to dispatch to its appropriate folder.

Once you've organized your existing e-mails, you'll probably feel a huge sense of relief. Now you know that your virtual in-box is truly an in-box...it's not a rest stop anymore. Keeping a clear virtual in-box is just as important as keeping a clear desktop.

Be Careful...

It's important to remember that as you create an organized workspace and an organized mind, you are putting things away. Don't let yourself fall into the trap of never reviewing your system – this completely defeats its purpose. Simply because your conscious mind isn't being reminded of something does not mean that your subconscious has forgotten it...it's still gnawing on all those loose ends.

Review regularly. This, for some, is the hardest part of staying on top of things, but once you develop a routine it will begin to feel very natural. Review your system on a daily or weekly basis, whatever works best for you. Some need to review hourly. Develop a routine you trust and stick with it.

Project Reminder Organization

Remember that everything in your life which requires more than a single next step is a project. Chances are good that you have quite a few of these.

You can create a projects file in whichever context works best for you. This might be a digital file, a file drawer with separate files for each project, or a simple master list, written on a computer or in a notebook.

Your master list is simply a method of containing and controlling your projects. Think of it as an index, reminding you of all your loose ends. These are not next steps; they are projects. Reviewing your list will show you what you need to work on, and from there you will (in most cases) clearly see the next actionable step.

One List or Many?

Some people find that having one large master list works best. Others find it much more efficient to create sub-categories.

The following are some common ways to divide your projects list. As with many portions of this summary, your individual lists depend on your own life and career.

Personal and Professional — It's helpful, for many, to divide their lists into personal tasks (plan garage sale) and professional (new office location). Remember that your personal list is just as important as your professional list. If you're overwhelmed by tasks at home, how can you concentrate on work?

Projects You've Delegated — If you have a large number of delegated tasks, keeping them separated might be a good idea. This will allow you to track these projects, keeping an eye on their progress, without letting them interfere with your own work.

Varying Projects — This category is rather vague, but if you have a lot of different types of projects, it can significantly help to organize them separately. For example, if you have a great deal of client-oriented projects as well as several office-oriented ones, separating the categories will allow you to work on each with greater focus.

Remember that how you organize your system is nowhere near as important as trusting and reviewing your system regularly.

Project Materials

These materials are only resources. They are not reminders or actions, so don't use them as such. Your resource materials are likely very bulky — not ideal for a quick reminder. They should be labeled, filed and stored away.

Random Input

If you're like many people, you probably have a great deal of very random information and resource material in your life. This can range from a magazine page featuring a home improvement you'd like to make to a thought created during a road trip. Regardless of their format, these items are just as valuable as an organized binder – they're just a bit trickier to organize.

The simplest way to organize this random input is to make a note of it. Ideally, this should be done as soon as possible, so you don't lose any thoughts. Remember that with a trusted organizational system, there's no need to lose a thought – ever! Later, when you have the time, you can transfer that quick note into the appropriate file. This might be your "someday" file, or it might be related to an existing project.

Some of the very best ideas come to us at odd moments, so never downplay the importance of random input.

Organizing No-Action Material

Plenty of good and valuable information has no action attached to it. The following are some common ways to organize this material. Choose the method(s) which work best for you.

Files for General Reference – These can be paper files, e-mail folders, or both.

Dedicated-General Files – For general reference materials which relate to a single, large project.

Contacts – For phone numbers, e-mail addresses, home addresses, and any other personal information you need to keep handy. Any current smartphone makes storing this type of information wonderfully simple.

Libraries – Remember to only keep what you need. An example of a library would be a collection of current and relevant user manuals for your gadgets.

Your Someday File

Think of this as your "fun file." Include everything you might want to do or see in the future. Remember that getting things off your mind is the goal. Include everything from a language you want to learn to a trip you'd love to take. Everything, big and small, can go in your someday file.

You can categorize this file if size or preference warrants it. You might create files for home improvement ideas, miscellaneous (ideas that don't fit anywhere else), vacation spots – literally anything goes.

Avoid the "Review" Trap

You may have created a "Review" file, and that's fine. In fact, it's great. However, be careful to avoid the trap of letting this file become a dead end. Review it often to get results, and toss anything that's become irrelevant.

Creative Calendar Use

We've reviewed the proper use of a calendar – due dates. However, this can be expanded upon to include reminders. For example, if you have an upcoming wedding, by all means mark down a date before the wedding by which you need to purchase a gift. You can fill up your calendar with this type of reminder, as long as each item is actionable and related to a due date.

Tickler Files

These files literally tickle your brain. Create a file drawer containing a folder for each day of the month, as well as each month of the year. If you need to be reminded of something, place the item or reminder in the corresponding folder.

This can also be accomplished in much less space by using the "reminder" functions available on virtually all current smartphone note and calendar apps.

Checklists

A very common yet underused organizational tool is the checklist. These should be used to remind you of goals, values, projects – anything. Checklists allow you to see what's important, as well as what's not. Develop the habit of creating these lists anytime you're thinking about something. It will give you valuable insight, create new ideas and allow you to eliminate some unnecessary ones as well. These lists should ideally be portable, but they can have their own file if you find it helpful.

Congratulations – you have, by this point, collected all your "stuff," processed it and organized it. What a feeling! Now comes the review process, which we'll introduce in the next section.

Reviewing – The Key to Successful Functioning

Setting up this wonderful system and then letting it just sit there is not productive. Unfortunately, it happens quite often. Your goal is to create a system which keeps you moving forward.

Your system needs to assure you that you're working on the appropriate things at the appropriate times. It should also assure you that it's okay to leave things on the back burner while you attend to more important items.

When Do You Look at What?

Simple as this question is, it can be tricky to figure out in the beginning. Remember that a very brief review is all that's needed to keep you on track. The trick is figuring out what you should be reviewing.

Your calendar should be the first thing you check. This will give you the day's outline. What absolutely needs to be done? Everything else must work around these time-sensitive items.

"Next step" lists should come after checking your calendar. Do you have an hour before your first meeting? Great. You're at your office? Wonderful. Pull up your "Next steps – Office" list and get going!

Remember that some days, your calendar will be so full that you won't have to review any further – all those appointments will let you know that nothing else can be accomplished. That's just fine – you've organized everything so that when you do have the time, your items and tasks will be waiting for you.

Updating – The Weekly Review

A weekly review of your entire system is highly recommended. Not only does this allow you to clear out things which have become unnecessary, but it gives you a block of time to process all the information which flies at you throughout the week. If you're like most people, you simply can't process every single item as it comes. There's just too much. The weekly review gives you time to keep everything organized. Knowing that you *will* do a weekly review relieves the stress that comes with excess information.

The following is a basic run-through of a good, solid weekly review. Customize as needed.

- *Paperwork*
- *Note Processing*
- *Calendar Review*
- *Clear Your Mind*
- *Projects*
- *Next Steps List*
- *Waiting Lists*
- *Review Checklists*
- *Someday Lists*
- *Pending Files*

The Best Review Times

If at all possible, try to review on a Friday, close to the end of your workday. This is ideal because the week's issues are still fresh in your mind, making you more likely to capture important details. You are also still at work, which means that many next-actions and delegations can happen immediately. Better still, a review on Friday allows you to enter the weekend with a clear mind, ready to relax and be refreshed!

If your schedule or career doesn't fit this model, simply create one which gives you these benefits, regardless of what day of the week it might fall on. Stick to this review period. The point, remember, is to create a system which works for you and which you trust.

Reviewing Your Life

Goals, values, aspirations – personal or professional, these larger items need review as well. How often you do this is a personal matter, but it must be done often enough to keep your mind clear.

Now that reviewing is understood, let's move on to what you're probably wondering about. You sit down at your desk, coffee at hand, ready to work. What on earth do you *do?*

Action-Choice Decisions

Now it's time to get real. How do you know, at any point in time, that what you're doing is the best thing to be doing?

The easy answer is this: You don't. All you can do is make educated choices, based on your stellar organizational system. This is why we've been stressing just how important *trusting* your system actually is – it's how you reassure yourself that you're not wasting time and effort. In the simplest terms, your decisions on which actions to take will be guided by your system and based on your intuition.

There are three main ways to frame your priorities. Which you use will be determined, of course, by your individual needs and circumstances

Four Questions for Choosing Actions

Action Context – Where are you? Remember that you have lists of actions which can only be completed in certain places, such as home or the office. This shows you what you can get done based on where you are.

How Much Time You Have – Obviously, a full-scale review of your system can't be completed during a quick breather between meetings. Fill this time with small, two-minute next-actions instead.

Your Own Energy Level – You're absolutely exhausted after work, and looking to be productive on the train ride home. Is this the time to draft a crucial proposal to your biggest client? No. This is a time for actions which don't require much energy, physically or mentally.

Priorities – Once the first three of these questions are answered, you'll be left with choices. This is where intuition comes into play. Which is most important? Only you can decide. Trust your gut.

Three Stages of Daily Work

These stages are what make up a typical workday for most people. The way you maneuver through the stages is, not surprisingly, based on intuition.

On a typical day, you will move back and forth between performing *established tasks,* tending to *new demands* and *defining* the work itself. This isn't as confusing as it might sound.

Imagine that you arrive at work and go directly to an early meeting, which you had marked on your calendar. This is an established task. After the meeting, your assistant alerts you to an issue at one of your branches – a very unhappy customer is demanding to speak with somebody high up on the food chain and guess what…That's you.

Of course, this is an urgent situation which you must deal with immediately. Once the customer is dealt with, you begin to process the e-mails which you've received since the last time you checked. Processing and organizing those e-mails is defining your work.

39

Trust your instincts and go with the flow. As long as you have a trusted organizational system in place, and you review and update that system as often as needed, no emergency can throw you too far off.

Living in the Moment while Avoiding Insanity

Interruptions are always going to pop up. They are a fact of life, and no amount of planning or organizing can prevent them or make them go away.

The zone-like approach to work (and life) doesn't require you to control interruptions. It's not possible. It requires, however, that you control how you *react* to those interruptions. Trust your system — you've set it up to help keep you on top of things. Work with it properly, and it will do its job.

Picture your day as flowing, instead of a series of immovable blocks of time. Stuck on hold during a phone call you didn't expect? Review your next-actions list. Did the meeting let out early? Don't stop to chat if you don't have time...use those "stolen" minutes to get something done. Being flexible is one of the main "tricks" of living a relaxed and productive life.

Six Levels of "Hovering"

The hover model is all about taking a look at different levels of thinking. Imagine you're in a helicopter, slowly rising above your life. Different levels of thinking occur at different heights.

After reading the descriptions of each level, you can decide for yourself whether a top-down or bottom-up approach works best for you. Remember that the vast majority of people find that routinely flipping their perspectives is the most natural way to operate.

Level Six – Time to get philosophical. What defines your life? Who are you, and who do you want to become? Personally and professionally, having these goals clearly defined can make many day-to-day decisions surprisingly simple. If you're stuck on a particular decision, you can "level up" and ask yourself if this action is moving you toward a life goal, or away from one.

Level Five – Goals are getting more defined. Where a level four goal might be something like "Open a new store in X suburb," that goal was spawned by a level five goal such as "Expand business in new areas." Generally planning for several years out.

Level Four – Getting even more defined, this level takes a look at your goals within one to two years from now. You may be planning and brainstorming, but the end results are still rather far off.

Level Three – This level is about your present responsibilities. This includes personal and professional duties.

Level Two – Representing your projects, this level is very grounded in the here-and-now.

Ground Level – This level is all about your daily actions. Make sure your "Next Steps" list is complete, which should typically contain at least several dozen next steps.

There are a few key points to keep in mind when approaching the level method. Remember that a top-down approach might seem ideal, but it's actually very difficult, if not impossible, to move toward top-level goals when bottom-level actions are not effectively managed.

Keep your job in mind at all times. This is not limited to your career. What is your job at home? At work? In a relationship? If your job is not clear, making even the smallest decisions can become overwhelming. Clarifying your job and responsibilities creates easier and more defined decision-making possible.

Top-level thinking can be confusing, but it's crucial. If you're uncomfortable in the path your life is taking, everything will feel wrong, no matter how well-organized you become.

A Quick Exercise

For many, simply reading about the different levels of thinking generates some interesting ideas. Take a moment, right now, to write down any thoughts. Process those notes accordingly before moving on.

Done? Great! Now it's time to review your vertical thinking.

Controlling Your Projects

So far, you've learned how to control and organize your items, thoughts and projects while acting intuitively, trusting your gut and trusting your system to keep everything under control.

Now, it's time to think about project planning. This is also known as vertical thinking, or fleshing out an idea until it becomes an actionable plan full of next-steps and concrete goals.

Why Informal Planning is Better

Pressured, formal planning is often encouraged and required in the workplace. However, if you hate it, you're in good company. It feels unnatural, and so it's generally much less productive than it could be.

Which Projects Require Your Attention?

The majority of your projects don't require a great deal of planning. In most cases, determining the next step is all that's required. For example, if you need to plan your family vacation, your next step could be as simple as searching for discounted hotel rates in your destination city.

However, there are two distinct types of projects which do require more thought and planning. These are those which stick in your mind even after a next step is determined, and those which suddenly appear out of nowhere. We're not talking about projects dumped on your desk at the last minute by an overworked boss – we're referring to those spontaneous ideas which come to you, for example, while driving home from work.

If something keeps gnawing at you, there are steps you should take. The first of these is *brainstorming*. This is free-thinking with pen (or a keyboard) at hand. Once you've brainstormed, process all those thoughts into their appropriate files by determining their next steps.

You may also need to *organize* a bit more. Gather up all your notes, reference materials, and anything else relating to the project on your mind. If you can't do this right away, create a next step on your list which reminds you to organize at the next available opportunity.

If other people are to be involved in this project, you probably need to get them gathered together. If this is the case, an obvious next step would be to *schedule* a meeting or less-formal gathering to brainstorm together.

You might need to *gather more data*. This could mean doing web research, calling people, or scouting a location. Whatever it is, make it concrete and actionable, then enter it into your system to work on whenever possible.

Out-Of-Nowhere Ideas

With the proper tools kept close at hand, capturing random ideas can and *should* be done on a regular basis.

Keep writing tools handy at all times. Laptops, notebooks, and even large whiteboards can be essential in capturing these random thoughts.

Supporting your captured ideas is just as important as capturing them in the first place. Paper files, folders and notebooks, as well as digital apps and programs designed to help facilitate planning and brainstorming can all be extremely helpful. Remember to process and organize all these notes appropriately.

Application

Remember that informal project planning is just that – informal. Do it anywhere, anytime, as often as you need. Keep it fun, keep it simple and keep it organized. These guidelines will keep you far ahead of the pack.

Section 3 - The Power of The Main Principles

1. The Power of Collecting

By now, you've learned a great deal about implementing an organizational system, trusting that system, and using it to lead a more relaxed and productive life.

However, the benefits of this way of life go far deeper than mere productivity. They can change the way you live, view the world and view yourself.

Personal Benefits of Collection

If you're like many people, you probably felt an odd mix of emotions as you moved through the steps in this summary. A feeling of guilt or even disgust with yourself may have surfaced. At the same time, however, you probably had many moments of feeling free, in control and relieved. How is this possible?

Sources of Negativity

Understanding why you feel negative emotions is key to preventing them in the future. As you moved through this summary, you noticed many things which you should have done, could have done, but didn't do. This made you feel very negative.

Imagine that a friend makes a lunch date with you. Thirty minutes before you're scheduled to meet at the restaurant, this friend calls to cancel with no explanation and doesn't reschedule. How do you feel? Irritated, annoyed, a bit betrayed. Why? Your friend broke an agreement.

What do all the loose ends and unfinished tasks represent? Agreements you've broken – with yourself. It's really that simple.

How can you prevent this? You have three main options. You can avoid the initial agreement. This is not a bad thing; many of the most successful and happy professionals have developed a healthy sense of when it's okay to just say no. Over-extending yourself doesn't do you, or those around you, any favors.

You can also, of course, choose to follow through on an agreement. Simply put, just do it!

Last, you can negotiate with yourself. A re-negotiated agreement is not a broken one, it's merely changed. Reschedule, arrange and accommodate — whatever it takes to avoid a broken agreement.

When you feel a sense of relief upon collecting, processing and organizing all your "stuff," it's because you can actually see all your agreements! After all, if you can't remember it, you can't possibly follow through.

Remember that the subconscious doesn't forget. This is why many of us feel so exhausted. Did you plan to tackle that messy hall closet six months ago? For six whole months, part of your mind has been thinking about that closet, *every second of every day*. No wonder you're tired!

You can do one of three things to silence that inner voice. You can become okay with the idea of a messy closet. You can clean the closet. Or you can renegotiate that agreement, placing it in your trusted system of organization. Either way, your subconscious will relax.

How Much Do You *Really* Need to Collect?

Of course it feels wonderful when we remember a very small item, such as grabbing promised take-out on the way home from work. Every little bit counts. However, don't get stuck in the pattern of "good enough." In order to feel completely in control, and to approach your life and work with an empty, ready, alert mind, you need to collect *everything*. Don't sell yourself short; you can do it, and you deserve it.

Expanding Collection Habits

Ideally, everybody in your life should try the steps in this summary. If you have the authority to get this started, you will truly be amazed at the results.

However, not all of us have that authority. Remember that for every member of your team who is not organized, you're losing time and money. Hint, pass this summary resource around, and try to teach the principles you've learned.

If all you can do is streamline *your* life, you're still way ahead of the pack. Even if the office is scrambling frantically around you, you'll know that all of your tasks and actions are organized and on schedule.

2. The Power of Next-Steps

Developing a next-step mentality has the power to change your life. As soon as you adopt this as a regular part of your life, you'll notice an immediate increase in focus, clarity, energy and productivity.

Though it's a very simple question, startlingly few individuals or organizations use it with any regularity. Once you adopt it, be prepared for some frustration. Dealing with people who have not adopted the next-step mindset can be annoying, even if you're dealing with somebody much higher up on the ladder than yourself. You'll likely look at them, their frustration and their workload – and wonder why they haven't tried this amazingly simple system.

Learn to pass on what you can, and let the rest go. You can't change the world. You can, however, make monumental changes in your own world.

Why So Powerful?

How can something so simple be so overwhelmingly powerful? The power lies in the simplicity itself.

Think of your lists. How long did it take you to come up with next-steps for most items? If you're like most people, only a few seconds. How long had you put off those few seconds of focused concentration? Weeks? Months? Years?

Only when you were taught a new way did you realize the power of next-steps. While it's a natural thought process, it's one that has been schooled right out of us by years of poor instruction and example.

What are the most essential keys to mastering a relaxed and productive lifestyle? Recognize action and separate it from thinking. Organize a system which you trust implicitly. Yes, it really is that simple.

Thankfully, these techniques can be learned quickly. They can also be improved upon every single day, just as any skill becomes naturally better over time with dedication and practice.

Why haven't we thought this up on our own? And why do some of us learn, then forget? The answer is twofold. We haven't thought it up because we've been conditioned to look for a more complicated way, a more sophisticated way. We forget – in almost all cases – because we allow ourselves to settle back into thinking instead of doing.

You Are Not Stupid

You may be feeling that way, once confronted with all you've let slide. In reality, the opposite is true. People who are not exceedingly bright or creative don't usually procrastinate. They push forward on a task, never stopping to think about the potential negative outcomes.

Intelligent and creative people, on the other hand, have a hard time *ignoring* the potential negative outcomes. Think about it. When you picture a high-level meeting with a very important potential client, do you automatically picture an outstanding, positive result? Do you picture securing the account while impressing the client, your boss and your boss's boss?

Of course not! You probably picture everything that could possibly go wrong, from forgetting the client's name to spilling coffee all over her pricey designer skirt. Is it any wonder you've avoided thinking about this meeting? It sounds horrible!

Realizing that you are jumping to negative conclusions is half the battle. The other half? Stopping. Go ahead and visualize the best, most amazingly positive outcome possible.

Identifying next-steps is actually dumbing down the situation. These smaller steps are easier to manage, which, in turn, makes the entire project/meeting/presentation much less intimidating.

Four Core Benefits

The following are the most dramatic improvements you'll notice upon implementing a next-step method of decision-making. With them, you and your co-workers become:

Clear & Focused – When you can identify what to do next, you have a clear task.

Accountable – When you have that clear task, there's no excuse for not getting it done. Excuses breed procrastination.

Productive – With their steps clearly defined, the vast majority of workers get more done in less time.

Empowered – Perhaps the greatest benefit of all, empowerment comes when you realize that you have the power to get things done. After (in many cases) a lifetime of feeling useless and bogged down in detail, this is a truly amazing feeling. It's also a feeling that will flow over into every aspect of your life, with wonderful and unexpected results.

3. The Power of Outcome Visualization

Outcome visualization, as long as the visualization is positive, is actually just positive thinking. This method of thinking has been hailed for centuries as the single best way to lead a happy and productive life. What have all those years of research taught us? It really does work!

Focus and Results

How dramatically and quickly these positive changes can occur has been demonstrated many times over by those who apply the steps outlined in this summary. Not only can they lead to more productive workdays, but they reach into every aspect of life. They can result in new and better jobs, an increased enjoyment of recreation, and a deep satisfaction with life itself.

Sound too good to be true? The only way to find out is to try, and it costs you nothing but a bit of focused time.

Realizing the Significance

What you've just learned will likely have results you're not expecting. Positive results. Our thinking is all connected; there's no escaping it. We can't determine what to do next until we have a clear picture of the desired outcome. Likewise, our outcome visualization is not realistic until we can define steps to take in order to make it a reality.

Everything which registers in your mind as "incomplete" must have a concrete link to "complete." Without this link, we literally don't know what we're doing.

Don't Ignore the Mundane

Remember to give small details of daily life the same attention as large work-related projects. Those small details make up the fabric of life, and ignoring them often results in a large disconnect. When you can think about, organize and control both small and large projects in harmony, you will truly become the master of your own life.

Natural Planning

Why should you just toss out what you've been taught for years? Simply because it doesn't work. When you adopt a natural-planning method, you'll discover that it applies to anything and everything in your life. Your thought process will become more integrated, you will feel and act more flexible and all the radically different portions of your life will seem wonderfully cohesive.

Parting Thoughts

Remember that these steps take time to fully incorporate. Practice patience and dedication. You will feel a rush identifying just one step — hold on to that feeling for motivation.

Work through this process as quickly as you can without rushing anything. Take the time you need, but don't procrastinate.

Teach others what you've learned. Not only will this contribute to a great work and home environment, but it will teach you new things in the process!

Revisit steps and sections as needed. This is a process. You have all you need, so get out there, implement your new knowledge, and get ready for a great life in the zone!

Made in the USA
Lexington, KY
25 July 2012